Batak Toba – English
PHRASEBOOK AND DICTIONARY

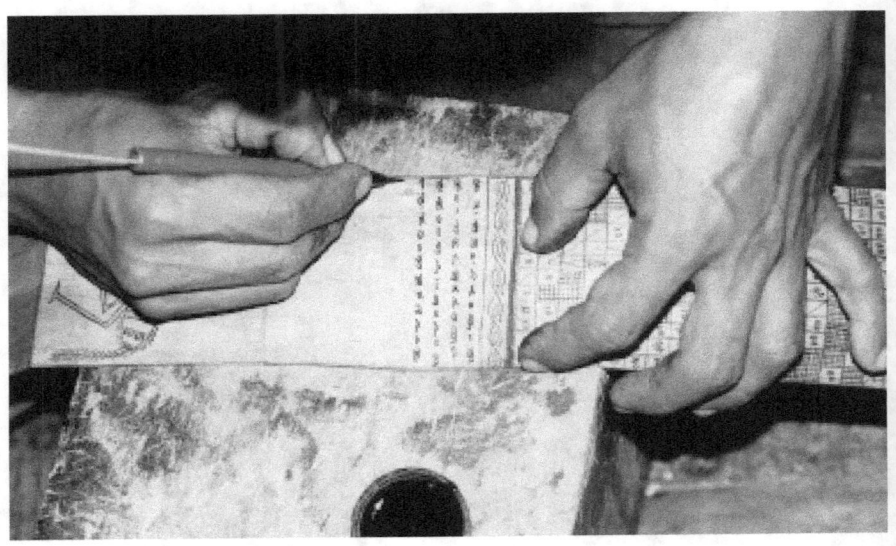

2

Lesson 1: Basics

VOCABULARY AND PRACTICE

yes – olo
no – daong

excuse me – sattabi, parmisi
baby (before baptism) – ucok
boy – baowa
girl – borua
book – sijahaon
heavy – borat
here (at this place) – dison
there (at that place) – disai

PRONOUNS

I – ahu
You (sg.) – ho, ko
He – ibana
She – ibana
We (inclusive) – hita
We (exclusive) – hami
You (pl.) – hamu sudena, hamuna
They – halaki

4

TIME INDICATORS

> **grammar note**: as there are no verb tenses a time indicator must always be used unless otherwise implied by the context

already – nunga
yesterday – nattoari
now – songonari
later (future time) – annon
today (already) – sadarion
tomorrow – marsogot
not yet – daong-dope

KEY VERBS

> **grammar note**: some (not all) verbs have 'common' shorter versions, e.g. *mamereng* becomes *bereng*, *mangida* becomes *ida* [see example 8b]

to **see** – mamereng, mangida

to **walk** – mardalan

to **find** – mandapot ,dapot

to **come** – ro

to **return** – mulak

to **name** – goar

to **know** – mamboto[want to know], huboto [already know]

example 1a: **ndang huboto**
                 I don't know.
    1b: **takkuboto**
                 I don't know.

to **read** – manjaha

2:    **ahu manjaha sijahaon saonari**
                 I am reading a book now.

to **leave** – lao

to **want** – laho

3:    **(ahu) laho tu Parapat**
                 (I) want to go to Parapat.

---

grammar note: a modifying verb (e.g., *laho*) comes after the main verb in Batak

---

VERBAL INFLECTIONS

---

grammar note: like Malay-Indonesian (or Spanish) **the pronoun can be indicated with a verbal inflection.**

verbal inflection:	-hu	I
	-mu	you
	-ta	we
	-na	he, she
	-ni halakki	they

to **search** – mangalului

example 4a: **lului jolo sada galas**
        You go look for a glass.

reply: **nunga dapothu** (dapot + hu)
        I found it.

reply: **nunga dapotmu** (dapot + mu)
        You found it.

4b: **ibana mangalului borua**
        She is searching for a girl.

reply: **annon dapotni halakki do boruai**
        They will find that girl later.

DEFINITE AND INDEFINITE NOUNS

> **grammar note**: articles – the function of the definite and indefinite article (e.g. in English 'the' and 'a') is controlled in Batak Toba by a suffix at the end of the noun.

If the noun is defined, add the suffix (-*i*) [pronounced '*ee*'], (-*on*), or (-*an*).

-on – *this one*
-an – *that one*
-i – *that one*

---

examples: **di portibi on** (a Batak swear)
             in this world

borua on
        this girl (the girl is present)
borua an
        that girl (the girl is present)
boruai
        that girl (the girl is not present)

If the noun is undefined, do not add anything (--)

example 5a: **songonari nunga dapotna**
               Now, he/she finds something..
5b: **songonari dapotna sijahaoni**
       Now, he/she finds that book.

PRACTICE CONVERSATION

ise goarmu ?
What's your name ?

reply: **goarhu si (Mary).**
My name is (Mary).

na maringanan dison doho ?
Are you staying here ?

reply 1:   **ido, na maringanan dison do ahu.**
Yes, I am staying here.

reply 2:   **daong maringanan dison ahu.**
No, I'm not staying here.

Lesson 2: Asking questions

QUESTION WORDS

> **grammar note**: like English, questions are stated with rising intonation at the end.

> **grammar note**: most questions in Toba Batak add the auxillary verb 'do' (pronounced 'doh') either after or before the verb depending on the type of question.
>
> A suffix *–di* is added to the verb in place of
> *-do* in some instances.

Where – di-dia, hu-dia, tu-dia

example 6a: **didia ho saonari?**
> *Where are you (now)?*

6b: **hudia ho?**
> *Where are you going?*

6c: **hudia ho nattaori?**
> *Where were you going yesterday?*

6d: **didia do kamar mandi ?**
> *Where is the toilet ?*

didia do adong panginapan ?
> *Where is the hotel ?*

didia do boi berengonku musik ?
> *Where can I see live music ?*

When – andigan (present time)
     – nandigan (past time)

example 7a: **andigan do ho ro?**
                    When do you come (arrive)?

7b: **andigan do ho mulak?**
                    When do you return?
reply: **ndang hu-boto**
                    I don't know.
reply: **olo marsogot**
                    Maybe tomorrow.

7c: **nandigan ho ro?**
                    When did you come?
reply: **nattaori do ahu ro**
                    I came yesterday.

Why - alani aha

---
grammar note: 'alani' also means 'because' (similar to Spanish 'porque')

---

example 8a: **alani aha lungunan ho?**
                    Why are you sad?

Who – ise

8b: **ise goarmu ?**
What's your name ?

8c: **ise ibana ?**
Who is she ?

What – aha

What time – pukkul piga

8d: **pukkul pigado toko an marbukka ?**
What time does the shop open ?

8e: **pukkul piga muse do tutup ?**
What time does it close?

QUESTIONS WITHOUT INTERROGATIVES

> **syntax note: TIME INDICATOR + VERB + OBJECT +
> AUXILLARY 'DO'+ PRONOUN**

8f: **ro do ho?**
Are you coming?

8g: **nunga di bereng ho?**
Did you see (it)?

8h: **nunga di bereng ho baruai?**
Did you see that girl?

8i: **di bereng ho borua na di sai?**
      Do you see the girl?

8j: **bagak do ibana?**
      Is she beautuful?

reply: **olo, ibana baga<u>khian.</u>**
      Yes, she is <u>very</u> beautiful.

8k: **burju do baowai?**
      Is he a good boy?

8l: **sonang do rohan dison?**
      Are you happy here?

8m: **lomo rohan laho tinggal?**
      Do you want to stay?

8n: **sonang do rohan di pardalananmi?**
      Did you like the trip?

8o: **laho porlu diho miak bensin?**
      Do you need some petrol?

Lesson 3: Feelings

VOCABULARY AND PRACTICE

happy	– sonang
sad	– lungun
jealous	– late
bitter(feeling)	– migar
broken	– malengleng
tired	– loja

good flavor, delicious	– tabo
good at something	– jago
good attitude/personality	– burju

beautiful, **nice**	– bagak
beautiful, pretty (for girl)	– uli
handsome	– jogi
heart	– ate ate

PREPOSITIONS

for/to (for a cause/reason) – tu

tuau – to me
tuho – to you

in, at – di
if – molo

KEY VERBS

to **smile**	– mekkel
to **remember**	– mangingot,ingot
to **cause to happen/makes**	– mambahen
to **leave**	– laho lao

to **feel** (an emotional state)   – roha

Syntax note: ADJECTIVE + VERB + TIME INDICATOR

9a: **sonang rohakku sadarion**
          I feel happy.

9b: **Na late do rohamu natoari**
          You felt jealous yesterday.

Syntax: ADJECTIVE + TIME INDICATOR+ VERB

9c: **Ndang sonang dope rohakku**
          I don't feel happy yet.

to **like** – lomo

10a: **lomo ahu tu ibana**
           I like her.

10b: **molohu bereng ibana mambahen ahu mekkel**
            If/When I look at her, I have to smile.

PRACTICE CONVERSATION

11a: **alani aha lungunan ko?**
Why are you sad?
reply: **alani malengleng ate-ate**
...because my heart is broken.

11b: **alani aha malengleng ate-atem?**
Why is your heart broken?
reply: **alani hallet hu lao.**
..because my boyfriend/girlfriend left.
lungun rohakku saonari.
Now I feel sad.

Lesson 4: food and eating

VOCABULARY AND PRACTICE

hungry	– male
thirsty	– mauas
favourite	– lomo, lomoniroha
very	– (suffix) '*–hian*' added to the adjective
sipangan	– food
bread	– kue
rice	– idahan (cooked)
	– boras (uncooked)

<u>to **eat**</u> – mangallang, mangan

example12a: **ahu songonari mangallang kue**
I am eating bread now.

12b: **laho mangan ho ?** (informal)
Do you want to eat ?

12c: **nunga male hamuna ?** (formal)
Are you(pl.) hungry ?

reply: **olo, nunga male ahu**
Yes, I am hungry.

reply: **ahu songonari laho mangan.**
I want to eat now.

12d: **ibana nunga mauas.**
    She is thirsty.

12e: **tabo do sipanganoni?**
    Is the food delicious?

12f: **sipangan on tabohian.**
    This food was very delicious.

12g: **sipanganon aha lomoni rohani ?**
    What is your favorite food ?

12h: **lomo do rohan sipanganoni?**
    Did you like the meal?

Lesson 5: Amounts

VOCABULARY AND PRACTICE

how many	– piga halak
how long	– piga leleng
child (sg./pl.)	– dakdak
baby	– gelleng
age	– umurna
years	– tahun
months	– bulan

example 13: **nunga piga leleng ho di indonesia ?**
              How long have you been in Indonesia?

reply: **sada bulan**
        one month

NUMBERS

one	– sada
two	– dua
three	– tolu
four	– opat
five	– lima
six	– onom
seven	– pitu
eight	– walu
nine	– sia
ten	– sappulu
eleven	– sappulu sada
twelve	– sappulu dua

example 14a: **sadia umurna ?**
>*How old is she ?*

14b: **piga tahun umurni gelleng<u>mi</u> ?**
>*How old is your baby ?*

reply: **walu tahun**
>*He/she is eight years old.*

14c: **piga bulan umurni gelleng<u>hallaki</u> ?**
>*How many months old is their baby ?*

14d: **piga halak dak-daknaki ?**
>*How many children are there?*

14e: **piga halak ianakkon<u>muna</u> ?**
>*How many children do you have ?*

reply: **tolu dakdaknaki**
>(I have) *three children.*

<u>grammar note</u>: the suffix *–mi, mu, muna* **indicates 'you' (pl.) possessive '-your'. In Batak possessive pronouns are suffixes added to the end of the noun they possess and are similar to the inflections added to verbs indicatating the agent of the action.**

Lesson 6: Buying things

VOCABULARY AND PRACTICE

How much – sadia

example 15: **sadia on ?**
How much is this one ?

sadia sipanganonon ?
How much is this food ?

cheap – muranai
expensive – arganai
cigarettes – timbaho/sigare
money – hepeng

to **buy** – tuhoron

example 16a: **didia do boe tuhoronku timbaho ?**
Where can I buy cigarettes ?

16b **adong Marlborom ?**
Is there Marlboro ?
(Do you have Marlboro ?)

16c: **didia do boe tuhoronku pulsa laho tuhpku ?**
Where can I buy credit for my telephone ?

16d: **sadia hargana ?**
       What is the price ?

16e: **boido pinjamonkku hepengmu ?**
       Can I borrow your money ?

reply: **satabi, ndaong-adong hepengku.**
       Sorry, I don't have any money.

16f: **boasa ndang adong hepeng**
       Why don't you have any money ?

reply: **alani pogos ahu**
       ...because I'm poor.

Lesson 7: Ability

VOCABULARY AND PRACTICE

<u>to **be able/can**</u> – boe/i + verb
<u>to **help**</u>   – hubantu
<u>to **bring**</u>   – boanon

<u>to **play**</u>   – '*mar*' + verb root

     to **play/make a joke**   – margait
     to **play a game**   – marmeam
     to **sing**   – marlogu
     to **swim**   – marlange
     to **play** (a ball game)   – marbolo

example 17a: **ahu boe marlogu**
                 I can sing.

       17b: **boido hubantu ho**
                 I can help you.

       17c: **boido ahu marlange**
                 I can swim well.

17d: **boi doho margitar**
   Can you play guitar?

reply: **olo, boido**
   yes, I can.

17e: **boido ibana marlogu ?**
   Can he sing ?

reply: **daong boe ibana**
   No, he cannot.

17f: **boido boanonna sijahaonan tuau ?**
   Can she bring the book to me ?

Lesson 8: Speaking

VOCABULARY AND PRACTICE

quickly   – hatop
slower   – nanget
louder   – pagogo-on
a **second**   – satokkin (a very short amount of time)

<u>to **say**</u> – mandok

example 18a: **aha nanidoknai ?**
         What is she saying ?

     18b: **aha didok ibana?**
         What did she say ?

<u>to **hear**</u> – mambege

example 19a: **Ndang boi hubege ibana**
         I cannot hear her.

     19b: **Ndang boi hubege ho**
         I cannot hear you.

     19c: **boido pagogoonmu makkatai ?**
         Can you speak louder ?

to **speak** – makkatai

example 20a: **hatop hian ho makkatai**
You speak too quickly.

20b: **boido ho makkatai nanget**
Can you speak slower please ?
reply: **daong boi**
No, I can't.

20c: **boido au makkatai satokkin tuho ?**
Can I speak to you for a minute ?

20d: **bahasa asanaboi di hataonho ?**
What languages cam you speak?

20e: **boido ho makkatai tu parubati ?**
Can you speak to the doctor ?
reply: **olo boi**
Yes, I can.

AGREEMENT

olo, doahu
Yes, I agree.

toho doi
That's correct.

Lesson 9: Travel

VOCABULARY AND PRACTICE

how far – sadia dao

example 21a: **laho tudia ho ?**
Where are you going ?

21b: **sadia dao tu Pangaruran ?**
How far is Pangaruran ?

21c: **sadia dao siannon tu Ambarita ?**
How far is Ambarita from here ?

how long – piga leleng

example 22:   **piga leleng pardalanan tu aek rangat ?**
How long does it take to get to the hotsprings ?

<u>to **rent**</u> – sewa

example 23a: **didiado boi sewaokku kareta ?**
Where can I rent a motorbike ?

23b: **nalaho di sewahondo mobilon ?**
Is this car for rent ?

23c: **pukkul piga do kapal borhat tu Parapat ?**
         What time is the boat leaving to Parapat ?

23d: **naek aha do boi ahu taho tu Sibolga ?**
         How do I get to Sibolga ?

to **change** (money) – manukkar hepeng

example 24a: **Didia do boi ahu manukkar hepeng ?**
         Where can I change money ?

24b: **Boido tukaronmu euros tu rupiah ?**
         Can you change Euros to Rupiah ?

Toba Batak syllabic alphabet

CONSONANTS

VOWELS WITH CONSONANT 'KA'

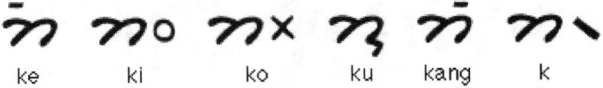

Dictionary

A

to **be able** – boe/i + verb
age – umurna
almost – laho
all – sude
also – dohot
always – torus
amazing – ulihian
and – dohot
to **argue** –martokkar
to **answer** – mangalusi, alusi
art – gorga
at – di
awful – hassitan, ngerihian

B

baby– ucok (before baptism),
    gelleng
bad – roa
bag – gajut
beautiful, nice – bagak
beautiful, pretty (for girl) – uli
because – alani
to **begin** – patwolo
below – jonok
beside – jenek
better – denggan
between – golakni
bicycle – lereng
bill/cheuque - bon

bird – andukur
to **bite** – mangkarut
bitter (feeling) – migar
blood – mudar
book – sijahaon
boss – tokke
boy – baowa
brave – barani
bread – kue
to **bring** – mamboan, boanon
to **bring** (a present) – marsilua
broken – sega, malengleng
to **burn** – manutung
busy – repot
to **buy** – manuhor

C

camera – tustel
can (v.) – boe/i + verb
canoe (small boat) - solu
careful – nanget-nanget
to **carry** – mamboan
to **cause** (to happen) - mambahen
chair – huudulan
cheap – mura, muranai
child (sg./pl.) – dakdaknak
children – ianakkon
cigarettes – timbaho, sigare
clean – ias
to **close** – manutup
close (adj.) – jenek
to **come** – ro

to **cook** – mangaloppa
comfortable – lambok
community – huta
country – luat
crazy – rittik, senu, sedang
to **cry** – taritu
to **cut** – maneat

D

to **dance** – marjoget
danger – berbahaya
day – ari
dead – mate
deep – bagas
delicious – tabo
difficult – maol
dirt – abu
dirty – homur, hotor
distant/far – doa
dizzy – mirdong
doctor – parubat
dog – biang
door – pittu
down – ditoru
downstairs – ditoru
to **drink** (v.) – manginum
a **drink** (n.) – minum
dry – koring

E

early – gira
easy – horup
to **eat** – mangallang, mangan
eight – walu
eleven – sappulu sada
empty – kosong
end – sukkup
evening – bokni ari
everything – sude, sudena
excuse (me) – sattabi, parmisi
expensive – arganai, arga
experience – talenta

F

family – pamili
favourite – lomo, lomoniroha
fat – mok-mok
fear – mabiar
to **feel** (an emotional state) – roha
fever – mohop
fight (n.) – marbada
five – lima
to **find** – mandapot ,dapot
fire – api
first – parjolo
floor – lante
food – siallangon, sipangan
forever – salelengna
foreign – tondong,
to **forget** – mangalupahon, lupa
to **forgive** – manolsoli
free (no cost) – pere-pere
fresh – segar

fried – nanigoreng
friend – dongan
from – sian
fruit – buah
full – gok
funny – pekket
for/to (for a cause/reason) – tu
four – opat

G

garden – balian
generous – mala
to give – mangalehon
God – debata
gold – mas
government – pamarenta
greedy – holit
to grow – manuan
guitar – karunjet
girl – borua
good (flavor) – tabo
good at something – jago
good attitude/personality – burju
to guess – mandodo, dodo

H

handsome – jogi
happy – sonang
to hate – marsogoniroha,
    manadikkon
hard/difficult – maol
hard – karas

to have – napuna
hello – horas
to help – hubantu, mangurupi
to hear – mambege
he – ibana
head – ulu, simanjujung
heart – ate-ate
heavy – borat
here (at this place) – dison
high – tibbo
to hire/rent – pasewahon
home – jabu
hot – mohop
hotel – panginapan
how many – piga halak
how far – sadia dao
how long – piga leleng
human – jolma, manisia
hungry – male
to hurry – pahatop
hurt – hassitan
husband – tunggani doli

I J K

I – ahu
ice – es
idea – pandapot
if – molo
ill/sick – marsahit
impossible – ndang hurippu
in – di
infection – marnanah
injury – tarseat
intelligent – pistar
interesting – tarnonong

to **invite** – manggokhon
itch – narasaon
jail – hurungan
jealous – late
job – parkarejoan, parhorjaan
joke – parekelan
key – gombok
to **kill** – mamburje
king – raja
kiss – umma
to **kiss** – mangummahon
to **know** – mamboto, huboto

little – saotik
to **live** – tinggal
lock (n.) – makussi
long – ganjang
long time – lelenghian
to **look** – mamereng
to **lose** – hamagoan
loud – gogo
louder – pagogo-on
lucky – marnasip
lunch – mangansiang

L

lake – tao
land – tano
language – hata
last – naparpudi
late – parpudi
to **laugh** – mengkel
laundry – manussi
law – adat
lazy – malas
to **learn** – marsiajar
to **leave** – lao
left – hambirang
less – hurang
letter – govetan
liar – pangototoi
life – mangolu
light – neang
lighter – loting
like/similar – hera
to **like** – lomo
to **listen** – mambege

M N

machine – masin
made – pinatupa
to **make** happen – mambahen
many – godang, torop
map – peta
to **marry** – mangalua
market – onan
maybe – oldora
to **meet** – manjumpangi
message – barita
minute – satiokin
to **miss** – masihol
money – hepeng
monkey – bodat
month(s) – bulan
more – tambu
morning – manogot
mountain – dolok
to **name** – goar
name – goar
never – nolang hea
new – imbaru

news – barita
next – sahalinai
next week – minggu nalahoro
night – borugin
nine – sia
no – daong
noise – gaor
none – kosong
nothing – ndang adong
not yet – doang dope
now – saonari

O

ocean – laut
often – jot-jot
old – matua
on – mangolu
once – sahali
one – sada
only – holan
open – bukka
to open – mambukka
opportunity – kesempatan
opposite – hata balikna
or – manang
to order/book – mamesan
original – has/asli
other – halakna-asing
out – kawar
outside – diluar
to owe – maminjam
owner – tokke

PQ

painful – hassitan
paper – harotas
part – bagian
party – pesta
passenger – sewa/paneimpang
passport – paspor
past – naung lalu
to pay – mambayar
peace – dame
people – jolma
permission – parmisi/santabi
pig – pinahan
place – inganan
to play – 'mar' + verb root
to play a game – marmeam
to play (a ball game) – marbolo
to play/make a joke – margait
politics – taktik
poor – pogos
positive – positip
power – hagogo-on
prayer – martangian
prefer – lomoniroha
present (time) – saonari
present/gift – mangalehon
pretty – bagak, uli
price – arga
priest – pastor
private – priyadi
probably – olodora
problem – sipikkiran
promise – marjanji
protect – manghokkop
province – propinsi
pull – manarik
push – mangunjor

question – manukkun
quick/quickly – hatop
quiet – sip-sip, pasisip

R

radio – radio
rain – udan
to **rain** – udan
raw – nasohona loppa
to **read** – manjaha
ready – nunga sae
reason – ulani, alani
receipt – bon, faktor
to **receive** – manjalo
recently – ipe-dope
relationship – pardonganon
relax – paulakgogo
religion – agama
to **remember** – mangingot,ingot
to **rent** – manewa, sewa
to **reserve** – paradehon
respect – pasambarhon
responsibility – tanggungjawab
to **rest** – paulak hosa
restaurant – kode
to **return** – paulakhon, mulak
rice – idahan (cooked),
    boras (uncooked)
rich – mamora
right (not left) – siamun
right/correct – situtu, sitohu,
    sintong
road – dalan
robber/theif – panakko
roof – atap

roam – mardalan, dalani
round – bulat

S

sad – lungun
safe – aman
salty – asin
same – sarupa
to **save** – manimpan
to **say** – mandok
scenery – panatapan
to **search** – mangalului
a **second** – satokkin
    (very short amount of time)
secret – sitabunian
to **see** – mamereng, mangida
selfish – siginjangroha
to **sell** – manjual
to **send** – mangirim
serious – marsitutu
several – piga-piga halak
seven – pitu
shape – rupana
to **share** – mambagi
she – ibana
short (time) – pukkul
short (height) – metmet
to **shout** – manjou
to **show** – patuduhon
to **shut** – mambodil
shy – maila
sick – marsahit
sign – manekken
similar – sarupa
to **sing** – marlogu

single (not married) –
  doli-doli (man),
  anakboru (woman)
to **sit** – hundul
situation – situasi
six – onom
sleep – modoni
to **sleep** – laho modom
sleepy/tired – tartuddu
slow – nanget/palan
slowly – nanget-nanget,
  palan-palan
small – tagelleng
smell/stench (n.) – bou, manggus
to **smile** – mekkel
a good **smell** – angur
some – piga-piga
somebody – sahalak
something – adongmai, sesuatu
song – ende
soon – sahatopna
sorry – santabi
souvenir – tokko ukiran
to **speak** – makkatai
special – khusus
spicy – siak
stack (n.) – marsitipahan
to **start** – mamulai
to **stay** – tinggal
to **steal** – manakko
to **stop** – pasitoppon
story – sarita
straight – lorus
strange – aneh, asing
street – dalan
strong – gogo, pirma
stupid – ototo
suddenly – soppong
sure – sitoho

surprise – adong mai
sweet – manis
to **swim** – marlange

T

they – halaki
to **take/carry** – mamboan
to **talk** – makkatai
tall – timbo
to **taste** – mandai
to **teach** – mangajari
telephone – talipon
ten – sappulu
thanks/thank you – mauliate
there (at that place) – disai
thick – tobal
thin – kurus
to **think** – mamikkiri, pikkiri
thirsty – mauas
thought – manurut
three – tolu
tired – loja
to (me) – tu ahu
to (you) – tuho
toilet – vehseh, WC
tonight – bodari
too/also – dohot
tooth – ngingi
torch/flashlight – senter
to **touch** – manondong, maniop,
  manjamah
tour – mardallan-dalani
tourist – tama, tondong
town – kota
to **translate** – manorangkoh

to **trek** – mandaki
trip – tirip
to **try** (a dish) – mandai
to **try/test** – manorong, manubah
two – dua
true – situho, situtu
trust – porsea
twelve – sappulu dua

UVW

vacation – lowongan
valley – ramba-ramba
valuable – arta naummarga
value – arta
very – suffix '*–hian*' added to
  the adjective
view – panatapan
to **visit** – martondong
village – huta
vomit – muta
to **wait** – mamette
to **want** – laho
to **walk** – mardalan
warm – las
to **wash** – manussi
to **watch** – mamereng
water – aek, mual
waterfall – binanga
we (inclusive) – hita
we (exclusive) – hami
weather – suassa
wet – maraek

what – aha
what time – pukkul piga
where – di-dia, hu-dia, tu-dia
when – andigan (present time),
  nandigan (past time)
who – ise
whole – lobang
why – alani aha
wide – luas
wife – pardijabu, inang-inang
to **win** – monang
wind – alogo
wire – kawat
wise – pistar
with – dohot
without – ndang pola
wood – hau
woods/jungle – hau
world – portibi
to **work** – karejo
to **write** – manurat
wrong – ndang sintong

XYZ

year – taon
yesterday – nattoari
yes – olo
yet – ndaong dope
you (sg.) – ho, ko
you (pl.) – hamu sudena, hamuna
young – poso
young man/girl (a youth) –
  naposo bulung

www.ingramcontent.com/pod-product-compliance
Lightning Source LLC
Chambersburg PA
CBHW070257300526
45791CB00022B/1532